Henry Littlehales, Catholic Church, Liturgy and Ritual

Pages in Facsimile from a Layman's Prayer-Book in English

about 1400 A.D. containing mediaeval versions of the Lord's prayer, Te

Deum, Magnificat, etc., edited from the original in the British museum, MS

27, 592

Henry Littlehales, Catholic Church, Liturgy and Ritual

Pages in Facsimile from a Layman's Prayer-Book in English
*about 1400 A.D. containing mediaeval versions of the Lord's prayer, Te Deum,
Magnificat, etc., edited from the original in the British museum, MS 27, 592*

ISBN/EAN: 9783337361136

Printed in Europe, USA, Canada, Australia, Japan

Cover: Foto ©Lupo / pixelio.de

More available books at **www.hansebooks.com**

PAGES IN FACSIMILE

FROM

A LAYMAN'S PRAYER-BOOK
IN ENGLISH

ABOUT 1400 A.D.

CONTAINING MEDIÆVAL VERSIONS OF THE LORD'S
PRAYER, TE DEUM, MAGNIFICAT, ETC., EDITED FROM
THE ORIGINAL IN THE BRITISH MUSEUM, MS. 27,592

BY

HENRY LITTLEHALES

RIVINGTONS

WATERLOO PLACE, LONDON

MDCCCXC

INTRODUCTION

THE facsimiles here given have been selected from a manuscript Prymer of vellum, written on both sides, and in a modern binding of brown leather (British Museum, 27,592). The book is unfortunately imperfect, leaves containing the Creed and other interesting portions having been removed. The greater part, however, remains, amongst others those pages containing the Litany and Ten Commandments. There are sixty-one leaves in all.

The pages reproduced are amongst the most interesting in the volume, and afford mediæval versions of the Lord's Prayer, Benedicite, Magnificat, etc. The only manuscript Prymer yet printed is that given in Mr. Maskell's " Monumenta Ritualia," and further information on the subject must be sought there, where the whole matter is dealt with at some length and with masterly ability.

The slight sketch of the Prymer in the following pages is, I believe, in great part an addition to that furnished by Mr. Maskell, as I have endeavoured in some degree to treat the matter from a different stand-

point. To Mr. Maskell, however, all notes on the ques-
tion of Service-books probably in some way or other are
indebted, as not only has he opened up the subject, but
contributed materially to dissipate the very strange ideas
which are to be found in works of earlier publication.

In the following sketch I have stated various opinions,
but as in every case I have furnished extracts and
references upon which they are based, it is open to those
who cannot agree with me to search for themselves and
to form their own conclusions.

Of the two pieces contained in the Appendix, the
first is from a book of prayers to be used during Mass,
and the whole of this manuscript has been printed by
the Early English Text Society, under the title of the
"Lay Folk's Mass-Book." The second piece is simply
part of a religious poem. Both are private compila-
tions, and therefore quite distinct from the Prymer.
They are reproduced from the originals of the fourteenth
century in the British Museum (Royal MS. 17, B xvii.).

The Prymer was a Prayer-book in English for the
use of the laity, containing the Calendar, Hours of the
Virgin, the Lord's Prayer, Ten Commandments, Creed,
Litany, Office of the Dead, etc.; and though there is
no other existing example of an earlier date than that
from which these facsimiles are taken, we may reasonably suppose that such books were in use in this country
throughout the Middle Ages.

The same book, when in Latin or partly so, was
known as the "Horæ," or "Hours of the Virgin," and

Prymers and Horæ did not, in their contents, differ very materially one copy from another.

The name " Prymer'" has been traced back by Mr. Maskell from the period of the Reformation to about 1350, and in so doing he has given extracts from various documents.   Several additional extracts of a similar character will be found in these pages.

The name " Horæ," or " Hours of the Virgin," may be explained in this way: Unlike the present arrangement of the services of the Church of England, those in the Middle Ages were not gathered into one book, but contained in several volumes.   One of these was the Breviary, containing the services of the canonical hours —that is, the day services, morning and evening.[1]

The arrangement of the Horæ, or Prymer, was very similar, the difference being that they were for the use of the laity, and bore special reference in their contents to the Virgin.

The Book of Common Prayer of the Church of England was compiled at the Reformation from the Breviary,[2] and, this being so, it naturally follows that a very distinct similarity is to be found in it to that in use as the Prymer in the Middle Ages.   This will be

---

[1] " due howres of ringing to service, That is to say to ring in to matens at seven a clock, To hie Masse at nyne a clock, To evynsong on work dayes at ii a clock, and on holy dayes according to the lawdable custome of the Citie."—Churchwardens' Accounts of St. Michæl, edited by W. H. Overall.

[2] The service of Holy Communion (or Mass, as it is called in Edward VI.'s Prayer-book) from the Missal ; those of Matrimony, Burial, etc., from the Manual ; and the functions of bishops from the Pontifical.

clearly seen if the pages here given in facsimile, all of which are taken from the commencement of the book, are compared with the first few pages of the Book of Common Prayer. Let us also bear in mind that our Book of Common Prayer not only took the place of the Prymer, but that laws were issued under various sovereigns for the destruction of all other Service-books, the new book being alone permitted to remain, and with such vigour were these laws carried out, that very few of the old Service-books of any kind are now in existence.[1]

The Book of Common Prayer, therefore, is a new Prymer, and in almost exactly the same way that it is used in church to-day, so was the old Prymer in use, or resting on the book-board of the pew in our old parish churches during service-time in the Middle Ages.

---

[1] "That all books called Antiphoners, Missals, Grailes, Processionals, Manuals, Legends, Pies, Portuasses, Primers in Latin or English, . . . shall be by authority of this present act clearly and utterly abolished, extinguished, and forbidden for ever to be used or kept in this realm, or elsewhere within any the King's dominions. And be it further enacted by the authority aforesaid, That if any person or persons, of what estate, degree, or condition soever he, she, or they be, body politick or corporate, that now have or hereafter shall have in his, her, or their custody, any the books or writings of the sorts aforesaid, . . . and do not before the last day of June next . . . deliver or cause to be delivered all and every the same books to the mayor, . . . to be openly burnt or otherwise defaced or destroyed ; shall for every such book or books willingly retained . . . forfeit and lose to the King our sovereign lord, for the first offence xx. s. and for the second offence shall forfeit and lose (being thereof lawfully convict) iv. li. and for the third offence shall suffer imprisonment at the King's will."—Statutes at Large, 1549, vol. v. pp. 342, 343.

"Articles of accusation against Morrall, Catline, and Sharpe, for hearing of Mass and keeping Popish books."—Calendar of State Papers, 1547-1580, p. 578.

"or he entur in to the churche, be it erly or late,
perceue all thynge for his pewe that it be made preparate,
bothe cosshyn, carpet & curteyn, bedes & boke."[1]

Mr. Micklethwaite, in his paper on " Parish Churches,"
in the *Archæological Journal*, vol. xxxv., speaking of
pews, says—

" They were widely spaced, and had large book-boards."

This remark is borne out by the appearance of our
Prymer, which from its size would require a large book-
board on which to rest securely. All Prymers, however,
were not of the same bulk, some being remarkably
small.

The following are interesting as referring to the
name and binding of the book :—

" All-so y wol that Thomas Rothewell have myn Prymour."[2]
" Also I will that she have my primer clothed with purpill
damaske. . . . Also I will that Ann the doughter of the said
Roberd have my primer clothed in ⁸bawdekyn."[4]

The next extracts will, I think, furnish fair evidence
that the Prymer was at hand in the bedroom, and in
use the first thing in the morning. If we bear in mind
that Chaucer's clerk would "levere have at his beddes
heede Twenty bookes clad in blak or reede," we may, as

---

[1] The office of a chamburlayne in "The Boke of Nurture," about 1450,
edited by F. J. Furnivall, Early English Text Society.
[2] Will of Richard Bokeland, 1436.—Earliest English Wills (E. E. T. S.).
[3] Cloth of gold.
[4] Will of Roger Drury, 1493.—Cullum's "History and Antiquities of
Hawsted."

it seems to me, reasonably determine that our Prymer has probably occupied a similar position.

> " In the morenynge whan ye vp rise
> To worshipe gode haue in memorie,
> Wyth crystes crosse loke ye blesse you thrise,
> Your pater noster saye in deuoute wyse,
> Aue maria with the holy crede,
> Thenne alle the day the better shal ye spede.

> " And while that ye be aboute honestly
> To dresse your self & do oñ your araye,
> With your felawe wel and tretably,
> .Oure lady matyns loke that ye saye,
> Ande this obseruañce vse ye every daye
> With pryme and ouris." [1]

The next extract is from a Prymer of 1534—

"Fyrst ye shall say in the mornyng whā ye do aryse from your bedde this prayer folowyng." [2]

In conclusion, I may say that we have seen that the Prymer, with its Lord's Prayer, Ten Commandments, etc., was well known in the Middle Ages—a fact which is not surprising ; for from a period long before the Conquest, the imperative necessity of teaching the people the main points of the Christian religion was again and again demanded and enforced. This may be easily ascertained by referring to the laws and canons of the

---

[1] " Book of Curtesye," 1477-8 (E. E. T. S.).
[2] Primer, British Museum, 1534, fol. 30.

Mediæval Church.[1] Consequently, the statement with
which we sometimes meet, that before the Reformation
the people of this country had but little knowledge of
those particular prayers on which so much stress is laid
to-day, is inexplicable,[2] probably having its origin from

---

[1] "And we enjoin that every man learn so that he know the Pater noster
and Creed, if he wish to lie in a hallowed grave. . . . And we enjoin that
every Christian man zealously accustom his children to Christianity, and
teach them the Pater noster and Creed."—Canons enacted under Edgar, 960
(Thorpe's "Ancient Laws," pp. 346, 347).

[2] "Const thou thy pater and thyn aue
　And thy crede now telle thou me?
　Yef he seyth he con hyt not.
　Take hys panawnce thenne he mot.
　To suche penaunce thenne thou hym turne,
　That wole make hym hyt to lerne."
　　　"Instructions for Parish Priests," about 1450.
　　　　　Edited by E. Peacock, E. E. T. S.

"Goodfaders & goodmoders & all that behere about say in the worshyppe
['honour,' see dictionaries of Old English] of god & our layde & of the XII.
apostellys a Pater noster, and Ave maria, & Credo in deum. . . . God faders
and godmodyrs of thys chylde whecharge you that ye charge the foder and
te moder to kepe it from fyer & water & other pelers [misprint for 'perels']
to the age of VII. yere and that ye lerne or seyt belerned the Pater noster,
Ave maria, & Credo, after the lawe of all holy churche."—From the Service
for Baptism, Sarum Manual.

"Pater noster, ave maria, and criede, leren ye chyld yt es nede."—On the
font at Bradley, Lincolnshire.

"Also whether your parsons . . . declare and publishe . . . the tenne
commandments . . . if he do not ye shall present hym."—Forme of the
Archdeacon's Charge, "Jones's Calendar," p. 129.

"It was neuer ordeyned, o good reder, without the singler prouidence,
and moste abundaunt grace of almyghtie god, that the multitude of christen
people shulde lerne by herte the ten cōmaundementes of almightie god, and
the beleue, called the Crede, the prayer of the lorde, called the Pater noster."
—Primer, 1538?

I may also add that children were taught the Lord's Prayer and Creed

a period when every endeavour was made to disparage
the Mediæval Church, and exalt the piety of subsequent
generations.

It is not necessary here to point out the strange
inconsistencies of such arguments. Innumerable evi-
dences remain both substantial [1] and documentary [2] which
clearly indicate not only a remarkably vivid belief in a
future state, but a deep religious feeling.

---

in school (see Furnivall's "Babees Book," p. 303), and that the Ten Commandments hung in certainly one and probably many of the churches in the
fifteenth century (*Archæologia*, vol. xlv. p. 119).

[1] Church fabrics, which were in use by the people constantly during the
week ("Lay Folk's Mass-Book," pp. xxxviii.–ix.), endowments, ecclesiastical
furniture, etc.

[2] Wills, charters, inventories, episcopal registers, etc.

PAGES IN FACSIMILE

Blessed be you amongst alle þi wymmen . and blessed be
þe fruit of þi wombe. R. Hali godes moder euere
maide marie . Bide for us to þe lord oure god. Paſt
ader oure þat art in heuenes hallked be
þi name . þi kyndom come to . þi wille be do
in erþe as in heuene . oure echedaies bred ziue us
to dai . and forziue us oure dettes as we forziue to oure
dettours . and leed us nat in to temptacioun . bote
deliuere us fro inel ɣ amen: Aue maria graca
plen marie full of grace oure lord is wiþ þe . blessed
be þou amongst alle wymmen . and blessed be þe fruit
of þi wombe. ihesus amen. And lede us nat in
to temptacioun . bot deliuere us from inel Amen:
Lord comaunde us to blesse þou maire of maidenes prei
for us to oure lord lecio piua . Sancta maria uigo
O ȝute marie maide of maidenesse. moder &
douȝter of þe kyng of kynges . solace us
þat we mote haue bi þee . þe mede of heuenlich
kyngdom . and wiþ godes chosen regne wiþ
outen ende . you lord haue mercy of us . þanke
we god . auteu: þou maidenhede and wiþ outen
wem . quot what preisinge I mai sei to þe . for hym
that heuenes myȝt nat take you beie in þi wombe .
Blessed be you amougst alle wymmen . and blessed be

of þe is risen þe sone of riȝtbisnesse oure god iþesu crist.
pray for þe peple bide for þe clergie · biseche for þe deuout
womankinde · lete alle fele þin help þat worþely mak
mynde of þee · ffor of þe is risen þe sone of riȝtbisnes
oure god iþesu crist. Glorie be to þe fader i to þe sone
and to þe holy goost · þe sone of riȝtbisnesse oure
god iþesu crist. psalmus · Te deum laudamus
þe god we preise · þee lord we knowlechen þe
vncles fader euen erthe worschipeþ To
þe alle angels to þe heuenes and alle maiestir þou
eres To the cherubin and seraphin crien wiþ vois
wiþ outen cessinge Holy Holy Holy Lord
god of ostis þe heuenes and erthe ben ful of ma
geste of thi glorie þe þe glorious companie
of apostles þe þe preisable noumbre of proph
et þe preiseþ þe white oft of martirs þe þe ho
lichurche knowlecheþ þorw alle þe world Fader
of riȝt grete maieste þi worschip
ful only sone And þe holigost oure comfortour.
Thou king of glorie crist þou art þe euer
les sone of þe fader þou were nat skoynus
to take þe maidenes wombe · forto deliuer man
kende þan þou haddest ouer come þe scharp
nesse of dey · þou openedest þe kyngdomes of he

nenes.to þeim þat bileueden in þe ... þou attest on
godes riȝt side. in þe ioie of þe fader. We bileuen þ
thou schalt come to be oure iuge ... þerfor we bise/
che þe help thi seruauntes. þat þou hast bouȝt
wiþ þi precious blood ... Make þem to be rewar/
ded wiþ þi seintes in endeles blisse ... Lord make
sauf þi peple. and blesse þin heritage. Gouerne
þem and make þem hie wiþ outen ende ... Ech
day we blessen to þe. And we praisen thi nam
in to þe world. and in to þe world of þe worlt
Lord vouche sauf to kepe us to day wiþ outen
synne. Haue merci of us lord. haue merci of
vs. þi merci be maad vpon us lord. as we han
hoped in þe. In þe lord. haue I hoped: let m
nat be schent wiþ outen ende. Ant Preie for vs
holy godes moder. that we be maad worþi to þe biheet
of crist. Iublaudibus. Deus in adiu...
... Od tak hede to myn help. Lord hie the
... to helpe me. Glorie be to the fader and
to þe sone and to þe holy goost. As it was in þe
bigynnynge and now & euere in to þe worldes of
worldes amen. Alla ... preiȝe þe lord. Diis reg ...
... o wrguede doþed. he is in fair here cloþed
... is þe lord in strengþe and he gride hym:

For whi he fastued þe erthe: which schal nat be styred.
Thy sete is greithed god fro the world þou art. flodes
lord lifted up: flodes lifted up here vois. flodes lifted
up here stremes: fro the vois of manie watres wonderful ben þe vpbarynges of the see. wonderful is þe
lord in hexþes. in witnessinges ben maad to be
bileued riʒt meche: thin hous lord bicomeþ holinesse.
in to þe lengþe of daies. Glorie be to þe fader and
to þe sone and to þe holigost. ps. Jubilate deo ois
Dieth to god euen erthe. serueþ to þe lord in gladnes
entreth in his siʒt in gladnesse. Witeth þat þe
old he is god. he made us & nat us self us. his peple and schep of his pastur entreth his ʒates in cumfort
as halles in ympnes schriue ʒe to hym. preiseth
his name. for þe lord is softe. his merci is wiþouten
ende. and in to generacioun & generacioun his tronþe.
Glorie be to þe fader & to þe sone. ps. S
God my god to the fro briʒt j. wake
puttede in the, holh manifold my ...
In desert loud wiþ outen were. and wiþ outen water
so in holi j. apered to þe, that j. seie þi vtue and þi
glorie. For betere is thi merci abouen lifes. my
lippes schollen preise þe. So j. schal blesse the in
my lif, and in þi name j. schal liste up in my handes.

Is wiþ grace and fairnesse fild be my soule· and
wiþ lippis of mirthe preise schal my mouth·þ҃. had
te mynde of þei in my bed in morwunges· I schal
penke on þe· for þou were myn helpere· and in
helmynge of þi wengis I schal be glad· my soule
cleuede after þe· þi riʒthond up toke me· þorlope
mo en þei souʒte my soule· þei scholle entre in to
þe lowist of the erthe· þei schollen be take in to
þe hondes of swerd· þei scholle be þties of foxes·
Forsothe the king schal haue ioie in god· þei
scholle be preised alle þat swerry in hym· for
stoped is þe mouth of wicked spekers· God ha
ue mercy of us· and blesse he to us· lijtne he his
face up on us· ꝛ haue mercy of us· þat we knowe
in erthe þi weie· and alle folkes þin helpe· knyn
nen be þe peples to þe god· alle peples be schriuen
to þe· Ioiful and glade be þe folkes for þou
demest peples in euenhede ꝛ folkes in erthe þou
riʒtest· Peples knowleche to þe god· alle folkes
be schriuen to þe· erthe hay ʒiuen his fruit· blesse
us god oure god· blesse us god ꝛ drede þei hym
alle þe costis of þe erthe· Glorie· þt· Anditote·
Alle werkes of þe lord· blesse ʒe to þe lord·
preise ʒe him· and ouhioʒe hi in euer more

Angles of þe lord, blesse ȝe to þe lord; heuenes blesse
ȝe to þe lord. Alle þe watirs þat ben aboue heuenes
blesse ȝe to þe lord; alle virtues of þe lord blesse ȝe
to the lord. Sonne & mone blesse ȝe to þe lord; sterres of heuene blesse ȝe to þe lord. Reyn & deuȝ
blesse ȝe to þe lord; alle spirites of god blesse ȝe
to þe lord. Fier and siþellinge hete blesse ȝe to
þe lord; cold and somer blesse ȝe to þe lord. Deȝes
& hoorfrost blesse ȝe to þe lord; frost & cold blesse ȝe
to þe lord. Yses & snowbes blesse ȝe to þe lord; niȝtes
& daies blesse ȝe to þe lord. Liȝt & derknesses blesse ȝe to þe lord; liȝtniges and cloudes blesse ȝe to þe
lord. The erþe blesse to þe lord; preise and oilȝeȝe
hym ly in ouʒ en eue. Hilles þope more & lasse
blesse ȝe to þe lord; alle þat uourioueþ in erþe blesse
ȝe to þe lord. Welles blesse ȝe to þe lord; sees & flodes
blesse ȝe to þe lord. Whales & alle þat mieueþ in
watres blesse ȝe to þe lord; alle foules of heuene
blesse ȝe to þe lord. Alle kinde of beestes blesse ȝe
to þe lord; mennes sones blesse ȝe to þe lord. Folk
of isr blesse þe lord; preise þei hym & oil hic hȝ
for euer. Prestes of þe lord blesse ȝe to þe lord;
seruauntes of the lord blesse ȝe to þe lord. Spiritus
& soules of riȝtfulmen blesse ȝe to the lord; holy

harpe ☉ preise ȝe him in tabour and croude preise
ȝe him in cordes and orgues. ☉ preiseþ him i cym
bales wel solbuyng. preise ȝe him in cymbales
of murthes. euen spirit preise oure lord ☉ Glorie
be to the fader ... as it was Antephn Wonderful
chaunge the makere of mankende. takinge a body wiþ a soule
of a man vouchede saf be bore. and so forth going ma
... seed ȝaf to us his godhede Cap. aj ana ligo.

ne mair euere be glad þat deseruedest to
... crist maker of heuene and of erthe.
... wombe þou brouȝtest forth þe saued
of þe world. þanke þe god. O Gloriosa domina
O thou ioiful womman ȝere a boue þe sterres
him þat made þe of nouȝt þou ȝeue souke
wiþ thin holy breste. þat con ... ille dide &
were þou ȝewest wiþ holi fruit. entre þei as þe
puȝe in to sterres. þou art mate wiudolbe of
heuene. O þou art ȝat of the ȝere king and the
ȝat of liȝt þat schineþ briȝt folkes. glade ȝe of þe
liȝ ȝifen bi a mauie ... oie be to þe fader antcpn
God ches hure and forþches hure. B. And he maketh
lowe dikelle in his tabnade. þr. Benedictus domin.
lled be þe lord god of israel. for he hap
... bited a maad redepcioun of his folk ✓

And he hay reied up þe horn of heelþe to us,
in þe hous of dauid his child. As he hay spoken
bi þe mouþ of holy prophetes· þat ben fro þe world·
helþ of oure enemys and of the honde of alle
þat hateden us· & to werni wiþ oure fadres·
and haue mynde of his holy testament· þe
ooþ þat he swoor to abraham oure fader to зiue
him self to us· þat we wiþ outen drede deliued
of oure enemys houdes seruen we to him·
nesse and riзtwisnesse· bifore him in alle oure
And þou child schalt be cleped prophete of þe heiest·
for þou schalt go bifore the face of þe lord to make
redi his weies· to зife knowynge of heelþe
to his folk· in forзiuenesse of here synnes· be þe
entrailes of merci of oure god· in whiche he haþ
visitede us comen from on hiз· to зiuen liзt to
hem þat sitten in derknesse· & in schadew of deþ·
to dresse oure feet in to þe weie of pes· Glorie
be to þe fader & to þe sone· Antephona· þou glorious moder of god euere lastinge mayde marie· þat reclennest
to bere þe lord of alle þinges· And þou mayden aboue to зife
souke to þe king of aungels· haue mynde þou meke maide
to oure preiere and bire euere to crist for us· þat we
bi þi preiere mowe deserue to come to þe kingdom

uenes Amen. V: Schelt to us lord þi mercy. R: And ȝif
us þin helpe. Oremus. Oure lbe. Concede nos
famuli us þi seruauntes lord god þe pribe
þat we molbe be ioisful euere moir in helthe of soule
and of bodi and thoruȝ þe bisechinge of the glorious
euere lastinge maide marie be molben be deliuered
of this sorbe þat we han nolb t use euliliche þe ioie
bitly outen ende. Bi oure lord ihesu crist þi sone
þat liuey and regueth bitly ȝe in oonhede of god
þe holi goost bi alle þorldes of þorldes. A
Liete be to þe lord: Thanke be god. Antepl
Come holigoost fulfille the hertes of þi tribe seruauntes
and bȝten the fier of þi loue in ȝeu: V. Send out þi goft
and þei scholle be made. R: And thou schalt make neiþe
the face of the erthe. Oremus. prie be. Deus qui corda
God that tauȝtest þe hertes of þi tribe s
uauntes bi þe liȝtinge of the holigoost
graunte us to sauer riȝtfulnesse in þe same goost
and to be ioisful euere moir of his holy comfort:
Bi crist oure lord amen: Antepþou. Blessed truur
deliuere us saue us and riȝtliche us. V. Blessed be the name
of oure lord. Fro now this nolb and euere. Oremus. prepe be.
liuȝti bisip outen ende god. Omipt sempitne
þat ȝaf us þi seruauntes in knolbleching.

desir is feith to knowe the ioie of the endeles lline
and in the inzt of the magefte to worschipe the
oncheorne blessheth. þat bi the sadnesse of that self
bileue we be kept and defended of alle aduersites e
uere more. Bi crist oure lord amen. Antephona
Alle halben of god that ben frlalbes to penitentes of
heuene. biddeth ze for us to oure lord. R. Riztfulnen beze
glade and blithe in oure lord. R. And makeþ ioie alle
. . . . of riztful herte. oireu? Biere we. ouripo depar
. . bleche þe almizti god. þat bi þe merites
. . . . Epi moder and maide marie and of alle hal
. . . . we be defended from alle iueles. so þat þouz
here praiers we molben life peisibly in thi worschipe.
Bi crist oure lord amen. Antephon lord zif us pees
in oure daies. for ther is noon þat fizt for us bote than oure
god. R. lord pes be maad in thi vrtue. R. In
thi toures. oremus. we be . Orisonn. A
. . . . Dd of wham ben holi desires riztful . . . . .
. . . . and iust dedes. zife to þi seruauntes that pes
that þe world miзt norзt зife. so that oure hertes be зiuen
to kepe thi hestes. and drede of oure enemys be tak
from us. so þat oure tymes be peisible by thi . . .
tecħoun. Bi oure lord ihu crist þi sone. þ
þe and regneþ god by alle worldes. of wo

ns: and the treuþe of oure lord dwelleþ wiþ outen ende:
Glorie be to the fadir ...s it was. pf. Confitemini dno
chnuep zou to the lord for he is good: for in to
the world is his merry ...eie nolþ israel þat
he is good: for in to the world is his merry ...eie nou
þe hous of aaron: for in to the world is his merry:
eie þei nolþ that dreden oure lord: for in to the
world is his merry ...f tribulacioun ļ. called in to þe
lord: and in brede the lord herd me ...lord be helpere
to me and ļ. schal nat drede. what þing man to to
me ...lord be helpe to me: and ļ. schal despise myn
enemys ...etere is to trust in the lord: þan to trust
in man ...etere is to hope in þe lord: þan to hope
in princes. Alle folkes zede aboute me ...in oure lor
des name fo... am broken in hem ...boute goynge
þei zede aboute me: and in þe lordes name for ļ am
venged in hem ...þei zede about me as ben: and
þei brente me as fier in þornes: and in the lordes
name. for ļ am broken in hem ...I was putte and
torned to haue falle: and oure lord up toke me ...
strengþe and my preisinge is oure lord: and he is
maad to me in to helthe ...ois of gladnesse and
of helthe in the tabnacles of riʒtfulnes ...þe
riʒt hond of oure lord dide vertue: þe riʒt hond of

with anten euce. Psalmus. Magnificat anima mea
soule worsshipeth þe lord. And my goost
haad ioie in god whu helpe. For he loked
þe mekenesse of his haude maide. lo perfore alle ge
neraous scholle seie I am blessed. for he þ stre
wrth hath do grete thinges to me. and h
is holy. And his mercy is fro kinrede in
tes to hem þat þey dredinge him. he did þay
in his arme. he scatere proude men with þour
herte. he putte doun miȝtti men of þe
meke. hougric men he filde with gooues
he lete emptie. e tok up isrl his child þou
kinge on his mercy. as he hadde spoken to oc
fadies abraham and to his sede for euere. Loie
be to þe fader a to þe sone. a. Sancta maria succur
Swite marie helpe to wrethes helpe litil men in soule
to sauue to weps praie for þe ple. bite for þe clergie
bisethe for þe deuoute thomas kynd. Lord shelue us
in glory. and ȝite us thin helthe. Oremus. Praie woo
Graunte us þi seruauntes lord god we p
praye that we mowe be wisful euere more
in helpe of soule a of body, and þorȝ þe bl
seechinge of þe glorious euer lastinge maide
marie we mowen be deliuered of this sorwe

✠ in hi trolþ I ·
thurgh mekenes of þo holy gost ·
yat was so mild
be bryght i mary mayden chast ·
be come a child ·
vnder pounce pilat pyned he was
vs forto saue ·
done on cros & dred he was ·
layde i his graue
þo soul of hi went i to helle ·
þo sotie to say ·
vp he rose i fleschlye & feile
þo thryd day ·
he steygh til heuen wt woundis wide ·
thurgh his poste
now sittes o þon his fader right syde ·
In mageste ·
þeyyn shal he come vs alle to deme ·
in his manhede ·
qwyk & ded alle yt has ben ·
in adam sede ·
I bel I trolþ i þo holy gost ·
and holy kirc yt is so gode ·
and so I trolþ yt housel es ·
totte flesche & blode ·
of my synnes forgyues ·
if I wil mende ·
vp rysyng als so of my fleshe ·
and lyf wt outen ende ·
▓ft yat has at hande ·

Alaf þe mude ond pñles poñl
þi lif wt Chauyr to al ȝede
Ihū my lemman þou art so fre
ffor al þou dedist for luf of me
What schal I for þat ȝelde þe
þou askest nouȝt but loue of me
Ihū þi sod my lord my kynge
þou me askest ine noue of þinge
but trewe luf & al Byrkynge
And bof cryed ȝit Abece nuȝuȝige
Ihū my deȝe my luf my luȝre
Nul þe luf & p is ryȝte
Do me luf þe with al my nyȝte
And for þe mane deȝe & nyȝte
Ihū do me to luf so þe
þat en my þouȝt vpon þe be
With þi Abete euȝe þou loke on me
And myldelyche my dede se
Ihū þi luf be al my þouȝte
Of oþ þyng ne kepe me nouȝte
But þt I luf asuȝne þerbȝonȝw
And þou haft me so duȝd donȝw
Ihū al þof I synful be
Fa onȝe Raft þou aȝipuȝ me
no more onȝt I to luf þe
þt þou to me Raft ben so fre
oaþ mylde fre and gure
þay for me þou art ꝑfure

www.ingramcontent.com/pod-product-compliance
Lightning Source LLC
Chambersburg PA
CBHW021459090426
42739CB00009B/1796